The *Seven* *Keys*
to a
Successful
and
Amazing
Life

A Transformational Guide to Unlocking
Your Inspiring and Fulfilling Life

VALERIE DAVID

BALBOA.
PRESS
A DIVISION OF HAY HOUSE

Interior Graphics/Art Credit: Nouf Al Jama

Balboa Press books may be ordered through booksellers or by contacting:

Balboa Press
A Division of Hay House
1663 Liberty Drive
Bloomington, IN 47403
www.balboapress.com
1 (877) 407-4847

Printed in the United States of America.

ISBN: 978-1-4525-2172-5 (sc)
ISBN: 978-1-4525-2173-2 (e)

Library of Congress Control Number: 2014916060

Balboa Press rev. date: 10/16/2014

Contents

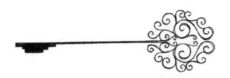

"You suppose you are the trouble, but you are the cure .You suppose that you are the lock on the door, but you are the key that opens it. It's too bad that you want to be someone else. You don't see your own face, your own beauty. Yet, no face is more beautiful than yours."

- Rumi

Acknowledgement

My inspiration for this book comes from the ever budding intention and desire for me to live the most amazing life possible.

I would like to graciously thank Ryan Cochran who has been my biggest supporter and confidant. He has always inspired me to live my best life ever. Ryan, I cannot thank you enough. Thank you so much for believing in me and my dreams.

Many thanks to those who follow me every Monday for Motivational Monday on Face Book. I appreciate your kind and enduring support.

Introduction

The desire to live a successful and amazing life has always been one of my deepest wishes. I can remember since my earliest memories that my life was truly special and that I had come to this life in physical form to do truly amazing things. My hopes and dreams would be crushed by several life events that I could not imagine would happen to me. All of these events unbelievable events would not stop me from pursing the life of my dreams. I would take my third tour to work in the Middle East and it was on this last tour that God literally brought me face to face with myself. I had just graduated with my Master's degree, published my first book, and had what I thought was an amazing year. But what I came to realize was that all my relationships were getting the best of me. Ryan and I were literally at odds with my decision to do another travel assignment. He did not think we could survive another separation. My sisters had stop supporting me and I was really at a point of devastation. I believed that I did not have a friend in the world. I really began to ask God why are things upside down for me? When everything should be right side up for me? It would all come to my realization within an instant. God whispered to me and said that your life is not turning upside down but indeed your life is turning right side up. I need to remove some things and some people from your life in order to create space for greatness; for your amazing life. And just as it had seem that things had gone really wrong for me, in an instant things became very clear to me. God spoke and I listened. It was time for me to be that woman that God had destined me to be.

It has been said that when the student is ready the teacher will come. It took me forever to learn this simple truth. When the desire to make a change in your life is brought into your awareness and you harness this desire with all your power and strength that is when the universe sends the necessary people, situations, and events to cause the greatest change to take place in your life. I mean it is so amazing when you begin to live the life that you are destined to live; once you do, you will wonder how you lived otherwise.

If you have a desire for inspiration that will change your life and you have picked up this book, my third inspirational book, be prepared to start living your amazing life. I am so grateful and excited to share with you what we are capable of achieving. The keys contained within this book will help get you started. Whenever we experience a shift in our consciousness and know the meaning of our lives we can never be the same again.

It is my sincerest hope that you will; like myself, begin to believe that you are meant to have an amazing life. You are meant to be happy, to have immense joy, to overflow with abundance, and to reach your highest potential. You are not meant to be small so stop acting small. Know that whatever you desire, desires you back. You carry the seed of greatness inside of you. I hope that as you read and apply each of these keys to your life that you will experience the immediate shift that will take place in your life. Faith is the substance of things hoped for the evidence of things not seen. All it takes is a simple belief in what you want to see manifested in your life and it is often referred to as the Universal Law of Attraction. Or as stated in the Bible, ask and it shall be given unto you.

This book is in your hands for a reason. There are no accidents in life. What you think about or whatever are your dominant thoughts are attracted you at an amazing speed. The practical applications in this book can be used to unlock the door to greater joy, love, happiness, hope, peace, and abundance. You are at this place in your life for a reason. Why continue to crawl through life, when you have the keys to your amazing life.

Imagine for a moment a world in which we all live in happiness and joy. That world is possible for me and it is possible for you. It only takes one person to start raising the consciousness of the entire planet. We are all inextricably connected to each other and so we each have an energy that is very powerful an energy that can be used for the good of mankind. Our thoughts create our realities in every moment. You have heard the saying, watch your thoughts because your thoughts become your realities, your realities your character, your character finally becomes your destiny. Thoughts are just that powerful, so why not choose thoughts that lift you and others higher. As we become happier and more grateful, those around us become more happy and grateful. This process then spreads so that the vibration of the world is changed and we all are experiencing the shift of our higher good.

These seven keys are your access to a greater awareness of who you are and what you can accomplish in your life. They can cause a ripple in your life and the life of those around you. Begin today, the process of changing your life. Start living the life that you are meant to live.

After reading this book always remember that you deserve to be successful and to live your amazing life.

1

The Key of Awareness

· ·

We meet ourselves time and again in a thousand disguises on the path of life - Carl Jung

The first key to unlocking your potential to an amazing life is the Key of Awareness. Start with the simple awareness that you are a divine creation of God worthy of any good and perfect gift. Awareness is simply the ability to sense all that is happening to us now and all that has happened to us in the past. When we become aware of our unique and divine nature our senses literally anticipate what is happening around us. Awareness therefore is the acute sense of mindfulness. It allows us to think about who we are and what we want, it allows you to process who you are and to change any aspect of your life. In that moment when we become aware of who we are and what we came to this planet to accomplish this is the moment when our lives begin to take on new meaning. We grow up in life being conditioned to fit into this person or that person, to do this job or that job, to marry this person or that person. Rarely are we told of who we really are what are true potential is. We are children of God and we have an amazing ability to do, be, and accomplish anything that we set out to do. We have been created to live an amazing life filled with love, hope, dreams, and passion. We just need to look within to the true awareness of who we are. A deep and abiding awareness of whom and what we are can set all things right in our lives as well as the lives of those around us. When you become aware of your true self and why you are here, ideas and creating anything that you want for your life begins to happen for you.

If you are overweight and have a desire to lose weight, it means you have brought this thought into your awareness and have thus set the process of losing weight into motion. Once a thought is brought into your awareness, you then begin the process or necessary steps to bring about or accomplish that goal. But first there has to be a complete awareness of a desire to change.

Eckhart Tolle in the Power of Now enlightens the reader about the magic of present moment awareness. Present moment awareness requires letting go of all thoughts about the past or the future and be here now. It requires a shift from anything that keeps us from witnessing the now. When we are aware of what lies within us, the power of what we can begin to manifest in our lives is beyond magical. Everything that we need in every moment of our lives is within our present moment awareness.

Most of us are asleep to the greatness available within us; in other words, we are on automatic pilot to everything that happens around us. If someone hurts our feeling we respond or if someone says something negative about us we take it personally. Awareness is a waking up from this sleep state into a higher level of being so that we can respond to all that is negative or all that hurts us from a place of love. How people treat you is their reality, how you respond is yours. You can choose in every moment how you will react or respond to people, situations, and events that are happening to you. To become fully aware of who you are and why you are here is truly the most amazing gift that you can give yourself. Awareness allows you to release the pains of the past, the fears of the future and allow you to lead a full life in the present moment.

The way to access present moment awareness is through prayer and meditation. You must let go of the conditioning of your life and begin the process of living in the moment. Release all thoughts of who you thought you were and become the amazing human being that God has intended for you to become. Awareness of your divinity will allow you to attract all that you want into your life. The blessings of joy, love, hope, wholeness, faith, truth, and abundance can all be yours once you are aware that you have a right to all of these things.

Forgive yourself for ever having the thought that you did not deserve all that is wonderful and great. You are meant to have an amazing life. You are meant to live life to the fullest and to enjoy all the things that you ever wanted to enjoy. There is no limitation to what you can achieve or accomplish when you embrace the simple practice of awareness. Remember that you are a divine being having a human experience. You have an unlimited potential to attract all that is good in your life. The universe begins to conspire to bring forth everything that you are thinking and feeling in this moment when your thoughts are in harmony with your awareness.

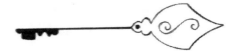

Apply the Key of Awareness

1) Begin today a practice of stillness and quietness. Release all thoughts about the past or future and just practice present moment awareness; because in this moment is where life happens. Life happens in the present moment so stay focused on now which is the only moment we have.

2) Let go of all thoughts that you may have of limitation and lack; and realize that what you seek is seeking you.

3) Begin a practice of knowing that you are and always have been perfect as you are. You made some mistakes in the past so forgive yourself and move on. Holding on to feelings of guilt or frustration is a waste of your precious life and consumes your present moment awareness.

4) Recognize the spark of divinity inside of you which allows us to dream and to achieve all that is possible to us.

5) Trust that what you want is already there only waiting for your senses to become sharper.

2

The Key
of Belief

· ·

*You can have anything you want if you are willing to give
up the belief that you can't have it -Robert Anthony*

The second key to unlocking your potential to an amazing life is
The Key of Belief. Belief is very powerful. I have witnessed entire
cultures dress and behave in the exact same manner. Our belief
about life, about ourselves, and about what we can accomplish is
truly important to what we manifest in our lives. You see what we
believe about ourselves and what is possible for us to achieve is
closely linked to our beliefs. The truth is if you don't believe you
can succeed, the battle for success is already lost. Whatever we
choose to believe about our lives will in fact become our reality. I
was repeatedly told that I would never be anything in my life but I
repeatedly told myself that I would do whatever I wanted to do. It
was my core belief in myself.

It is our core belief system that determines what we believe that we can accomplish. Our every thought shapes our awareness about our lives. A belief is something you hold onto because you **KNOW** it is true. There is nothing more motivating and at the same time nothing more destructive than the power of a belief. A belief can become your best friend or you worst enemy. The more aware you are of your underlying belief systems; however, the more powerful you will become to achieve your dreams and goals. Awareness is the key to creating that change. Awareness is the beam of light in the dark room of your belief systems. It breaks through the darkness, illuminates the way and allows you to move through your life with confidence and hope.

What we manifest in our lives is in direct proportion to the beliefs we harness about ourselves. They are the keys to an amazing life. The divine force that is available in the universe is available to every person. The mental conditioning that takes place within our families is what causes some of us to have limiting beliefs about who we are and about what we can accomplish in life. The simple belief that you can achieve greatness will start the process for greatness to occur in your life. We literally become what we think about or what we believe about ourselves.

One of the most important things we can do as parents is to teach our children a strong foundation and a firm belief that they are a part of something greater than they can imagine. They are part of the same divine universal consciousness that cause a flower to bloom in the spring time. We have to teach them that whatever they believe in their mind they can achieve in reality. The same is true with raising our universal consciousness; we have to start believing that great things are going to happen. We don't have to struggle over things because we are a part of something great, something divine, and something so amazing. We only have to believe in this power; the power to create, the power to change, the power to evolve. Whatever is our deep driving belief is what will be manifested in our lives.

Apply the Key of Belief

1) Identify one belief that holds you back from achieving your goals and dreams. Analyze why you have it, acknowledge that it no longer serves you and then destroy it.

2) Challenge yourself and start changing the limiting beliefs that you have about yourself and what is possible for you.

3) Take steps to increase your belief in a higher power that can help you to achieve the amazing things that are possible in your life.

4) Eliminate and destroy all negative self-talk.

3

The Key of Attention

. . . .

What you pay attention to grows -Geneen Roth

The third key to unlocking your potential to an amazing life is the Key of Attention. Have you ever had an unending desire to achieve a particular thing or goal, and most probably you desired it with all your heart? Have you ever had a desire to succeed against all odds? For example, if you want to go back to school to get a higher education, you will start by focusing all of your attention and energy in the direction of achieving that goal. As it is with anything you want to attract in your life. If you desire something bad enough you will place all of your power and attention on achieving that goal. You see energy flows where attention goes.

Attention is the deliberate act of putting a thing or thought in your mind until it becomes a habit or it becomes a reality. Just like the opening quote from the author Roth, what we pay attention to grows. It is impossible to think about thoughts of a happy and satisfying life and have a life of misery and turmoil. Life just doesn't work that way. The universal Law of Attraction is an unerring law and it states that we don't manifest what we want but that we manifest what we are. Your attention determines your reality.

Attention is also known as mindfulness, awareness, or concentration. Attention can be practiced throughout our daily lives to bring about whatever change we wish to see. If you want more moments of joy, gratitude, and happiness, place your attention on these things and they are sure to follow.

Take for example a gardener; he carefully plants his seeds into the soil, waters them and leaves them to grow. The same is true with whatever it is you want in your life. Plant the seeds that you wish to harvest and then allow them the space to grow. Plant seeds of greatness, if you wish to be great. Plant seeds of happiness if you wish to be happy. Plant seeds of abundance if you wish to experience abundance. Some days when I am out for a walk, I will silently bless everyone that I meet. Or some days while paying for my lunch, I will buy lunch for the person in the line behind me. I never expect anything back from these people but the most amazing thing will happen in return as I give out, I receive in return.

Your life will begin to be truly amazing when you start to focus on the truth of who you are; that is, your amazing divine self. Start by paying attention to the things that you want in your life. Pay attention to the things that you love. Pay attention to all the small things around you. Things liked the sun rise, the smile of a child, the gift of kindness, the bud of a new flower. When you place your attention on the small things in life you are able to witness the power of all great things around you. Placing your attention on the details of the smallest things allows you to take a moment of slowing down and processing all that is amazing in life. Take your attention off the things you don't want or don't love. You see where your desire is there is your attention. The power of attention brings everything to you that you want. Focus brings everything into perspective in order that you may place your attention there.

Take the Law of Attraction, it states, whatever you give out, is what you receive back in return. The Law of Attraction is so powerful that it works the same for everyone and it works every time. It is like a boomerang, whatever you throw out comes back to you. It is a law and laws cannot be changed or altered. If you drop something from the top of a building it will always go down, it is the same with natural laws. Laws are unfaltering; they work the same every time. Whatever we want to be, whatever we want to do, and whatever we want to have in our life is possible with the focus of our attention on that object. Wherever you place your attention the most becomes your reality. What do you want to happen for your life today? Do you want things that are positive, then start by focusing on the positive things? Do you want more abundance, then you have to start by focusing on abundance. Do you want more gratitude, then focus on gratitude. And finally, I have to tell you that if you want more drama, then continue to focus on drama and it will be yours as sure as the sun rises. The choice is yours. You choose in every moment. It will be difficult at first but if you stick with it, your thoughts must and will change as it is the law. YOUR IMAGINATION is able to do all that you ask in proportion to the degree of your attention. All progress, all fulfilment of desire, depend upon the control and concentration of your attention. Attention may be either attracted from without or directed from within. When you attain control of the internal direction of your attention, you will no longer stand in shallow water but will launch out into the deep ocean of life.

Apply the Key of Attention

1) Focus your attention only on the things you want to attract in your life.

2) Do not place your attention on the things that you do not want to attract because your mind does not care what is placed on its subconscious. It will only attract that object.

3) Practice focusing your attention on just one thing for an entire day. This will be difficult at first because the mind will tend to wander from one thought to another. But with your attention this application is possible.

4) Always place your attention in the present moment where the potential to create is the greatest.

4

The Key of Transformation

. . . .

Let the tears fall until there aren't any left. Let your heart break into what feels like a thousand pieces. For in this letting go, you are rebuilding yourself. In each ending there is a new beginning – Author Unknown

The fourth key to unlocking your potential to an amazing life is the Key of Transformation. Transformation is going beyond your form. It is going beyond the limitations of what you think you can achieve in your life. Transformation requires a completely new way of looking at things and a complete new way of being. We can't begin to create a new reality for our lives until we have moved beyond the old way of living and doing things.

Hospitals, banks, and many other types of organizations will all experience some type of transformational change. Most organizations realize in order to survive in the future global world that they must stay informed and find ways of expanding themselves. They have come to realize the need to make changes that will sustain their mission and vision in order to provide the best customer services.

The bible urges us to be ye transformed by the renewing of our mind. To be a transformed being all of your thoughts must change about how you feel about yourself and how you think about your life. Transformation begins with a willingness and strong desire to be different than what you are now. You must know that you are special and that you are here for a purpose; you must want to live an amazing life. Our lives as we have created them are a direct result of our thinking and we cannot change our lives until we change our thinking. Transformation does just that, it helps us to shift our thinking. We become what we think. So if we want positive things to happen in our lives we must have positive thoughts about our lives. If you think about negative things then negative things will become your reality. Now you may say that I think positive thoughts all the time, but the one negative thought that you might think can negate your positive thoughts. Positive thoughts and a new way of thinking must be practice daily. What we do on a daily basis becomes our habits.

Perhaps the story of the butterfly's metamorphosis represents the most familiar story of transformation. The butterfly larvae feeds on the host's plant leaves until it develops into a caterpillar later it will shed its outer skin before becoming a chrysalis. The chrysalis thus becomes increasingly transparent until the hidden transformation is complete and like magic the beautiful butterfly emerges.

The same majestic transformation can take place in your life after the process of the required inner work of letting go of the past and living intuitively in the now. The greater the outer change we wish to manifest, the greater the inner change we must take. Intention and desire to change must precede a willingness to transform. Affirm what it is you want to happen in your life. Say, I want to be healthy of I want to have a great relationship. Believe without allowing doubt to come into your life and start living your amazing life now.

Transformation is a process that can change your life forever. Place your attention only on the things that you want to manifest in your life. Attention is a process once mastered will allow you to manifest all your dreams.

Why live less than your amazing life? Why settle for less than who you can be? You have within you the divine power to create and achieve anything that you desire. You are a part of an immensely divine universe that wants nothing but the best for you. After years of searching, I finally made my leap of faith towards my personal transformation and my life has been amazing ever since. It was a hard thing to give up the comfortable beliefs and thoughts patterns that occupied my thoughts for so long. I always knew; however, that I wanted to make a change in my life because what I was doing was not working for me. Each of us must come to that place for ourselves and accept the fact that if you want a different life you have to make a different choice.

We have to be willing to come apart, to let go of our past hurts and pains, to allow the masks to fall off, to become the beautiful person that we are meant to be. We can acknowledge the hurts but we can't stay in them. You must take responsibility for where you are now, now is all we have, and therefore now is where true transformation takes place. Take an inventory of where you are now and where you want to be and then begin each day to let go as well as practice the steps outline in this book towards an amazing life.

The power to transform your life, your relationships, your family, and your thoughts are available to you at any moment that you are ready, it's up to you.

Apply the Key of Transformation

1) Real transformation is a process that takes place within your soul. Begin your inner transformation by placing your attention only on the things that you want or desire for your life.

2) Learn to be grateful for your past experiences but learn to let them go as they are in your past for a reason. You chose them and needed them for you higher growth.

3) Allow a transformation to take place in your life and emerge as the beautiful butterfly that you are.

4) Be willing to die to your old self and be renewed by the power of your mind.

5) Your amazing life awaits you; transformation begins with the intention to change. Place your attention on what you intend to manifested in your life.

5

The Key of Awakening

* *

Wake up, our ship has been ice bound long enough,
the time has come to sail the open seas –Rumi

The fifth key to unlocking your potential to an amazing life is the Key of Awakening. As you begin to awake from the dream of the planet and a life of planetary conditioning you can begin to shift into a place of personal fulfillment. Awakening requires that we let go of the past and anything that does not uplift and inspire us. As we awake a shift occurs in and around us. We become alive, those around us become alive, and the whole planet comes alive. Awakening is very powerful because your senses have been dull by society and the societal dream; the societal dream that we buy into as children who tells you to think this way or that way, play with this person and not that person. Well, I have learned to dance by the music of my own soul and it feels amazing to me.

Awakening refers to a state of waking up, wakefulness, and a state of conscious awareness. When you wake from your sleep you shift into a new reality about your life, you wake to the true essence of who you are. This shift is not something that needs to happen in the future but it can happen at any time that you are ready.

Awaken to your higher self, to your higher purpose and live the life you imagine. When you feel that urging within you will leave behind the shallow life of the past and awaken to new dimensions of your life; dimensions of joy, of hope, of peace, of abundance. There is no way that you can stay the same once you are awake to the real authentic self.

In order to move beyond the self-imposed limits that you place on your life you have to believe in the power of your thoughts to change your life. Inertia cripples us but action propels us to higher levels of ourselves and all that is possible to achieve in life.

The world that we are experiencing in our life is the world that we have created in our past. If we want a different world we must awake and shift our consciousness to a higher level and bring about the change that we wish to see in our lives.

When you finally awake you will wonder how you remained asleep so long. In this awaken state is when all that is possible for you begins to happen. Things begin to unfold almost magically and you begin to wonder how you have lived otherwise. Wake now to the magnificent beauty of what is your life and begin to live your amazing life. I can't say it enough you can have all that you want in life; amazing joy, peace, abundance, and love. It is yours when you tune into the higher consciousness that is in and a part of each of us.

Moreover when you are awakened you will realize that it is really you that have kept you from achieving what is possible for you. We have always had everything that we need to come alive. We are powerful beings with powerful purposes. Stop living so small, release your fear, and get on with your amazing life. Awakening to your life's purpose is the easiest way to living an amazing life because your inner purpose is to awaken to a higher awareness of what is possible to you. In whatever you choose to believe just remember that the highest state of consciousness is the awaken state.

Apply the Key of Awakening

1) Seek deeply within your heart until you awaken to your spirit.

2) Seek only those things that excite your spirit.

3) Lose interest in conflict and seek peace when you are dealing with others.

4) In every moment choose love without expecting anything in return.

5) Begin a practice of non-judgment. When we awake to who we are we have no interest in judging others.

6

The Key of Gratitude

· ·

May the Gratitude in my heart kiss the entire universe – Hafiz

The sixth key to unlocking your potential to an amazing life is the Key of Gratitude. When all of life is embraced for what it is gratitude becomes the magic key to your happiness. Gratitude is the most humble act of mankind; a grateful heart holds only to the highest form of love. In fact, you will find that the more you are in a state of gratitude, the more you will have to be grateful for. It does not collect wrong doings, it forgives easily, and it finds a way to make peace with those around you. The path to fulfillment is easy when we learn how to be grateful for everything that shows up in our lives. Gratitude gives us the power to love unconditionally and see past the faults of others. If you want to improve the circumstances of your life learn quickly to develop an attitude of gratitude. Gratitude allows you to develop the inner work necessary to transform your life. It allows you to turn weaknesses into strength, sadness into joy, sickness into health, and scarcity into abundance. When we are grateful we don't worry about the problems of the day because our thoughts are on how we can make someone else's life great. When you see life through the eyes of gratitude the world becomes an amazingly magical place. You are able to forgive your enemies, love those who have hurt you, and stay in a place of peace and wonder.

One day I decided to silently bless everyone that I met in my day; this was one of the most amazing experiences that I ever experience because all I did was simply sent out blessings to everyone I saw. The best thing about this experiment was actually how it made me feel. I had the most amazing feeling of thankfulness and gratitude. This process cost me nothing and all I did was send silent blessings to those I met in my day. If someone came into my office, I silently blessed them. Gratitude should never be an action to get something that you want but let it be an experience where you bless those around you and in blessing others you will be blessed.

Don't wait for moments to be grateful instead make gratitude a part of your daily life. When life is good, be grateful, say thank you and celebrate. When life is bitter, say thank you and grow. Not every day is going to be a day without troubles but you can; in each moment, choose how you will respond to the troubles of the day.

Keep in mind that gratitude unlocks the fullness of life and turns what we have into enough. The wonderful thing is that when you are humble and have a grateful heart the universe will conspire to bring you more of what you are grateful for. Again, the Law of Attraction states that, what we are is what is manifested in our lives. Thankfulness is showing appreciation for something that someone has blessed you with but gratitude is a state of being and it changes people as well as it changes the world around us. Cicero says, "Gratitude is the mother of all virtues".

When I first decided to write about gratitude, I thought like we all do that just saying thank you to someone was enough. Gratitude is much more than that. Gratitude requires us to think about the blessings in our lives, it requires us to be in awe of life, and it requires us to think of others instead of always thinking of ourselves. As we go through life we realize that we are all a part of something bigger and that we are all connected as spirits. Therefore we must treat each other with the love and kindness.

Learn to express gratitude in everything that you do and to every person that you meet. You will be amaze at the great feeling that you will have. Gratitude is the sign of noble souls; it is the key to your highest happiness. When you send out a higher vibration to the world you cause an effect to take place that returns in kind more gratitude. What you give out is what comes back to you. Send wonderful thoughts as it will encourage others to do the same.

The benefits of gratitude are many; you tend to be happier, people are attracted to you, you build better relationships with those around you, you are more peaceful, and ultimately you have more abundance in your life. Make sure to make gratitude independent of how you feel at any time. Make it a daily practice just as brushing your teeth. See people and situations less with your physical eyes and more with your heart.

Apply the Key of Gratitude

1) Develop an attitude of gratitude.

2) Express gratitude for an entire day.

3) Keep a gratitude journal and write down all the things that you are grateful for. You will be amazed at how these things seem to add up so easily as your heart shifts from your ego to all that is good in your life.

4) Be in a state of gratitude for everything that shows up in your life, be thankful for the good times as well as the trying times.

5) Practice gratitude awareness with your family, colleagues, social groups, as well as with those you don't know.

7

The Key of Love

- -

To acquire love, fill yourself up with it until you become a magnet for love - Charles Haanel

The Seventh key to unlocking your potential to an amazing life is the key of Love. Love is the most powerful force in the Universe. It is the cause of everything great in our lives. Love is a real force that can never be explained by mere words. Take for example; when you fall in love with someone, the emotions and feelings that your experience and express are unexplainable beyond words. Love is forgiving of all wrongs, love does not hold grudges, love is accepting people for the miracle that they are. When we love we are using the most powerful force in the Universe.

Love is talked about in books, written about in songs, and cherished by everyone on the planet in their own languages. It is the one thing in the universe that is enduring and everlasting. You can't see or touch love but you know that it is there when you experience it.

You know it when someone else tells you that they love you as well you show it when you tell someone else that you love them. In this simplistic example is the emotion of love but love is more than an emotion. Love is not just about emotions or feelings love is more powerful than we can imagined. Love is a force, a power that can change the world.

We came from the divine force of love, we are born of love, our entire make-up comes from love. The reason that we stop loving or can't love is that we have been conditioned by the opinions of our families and societies. We have lost the meaning of what this force of love really means. Again, Love is not just a feeling, love is a force. When you harness the power of love you are attracting the most amazing power in the Universe. Be in love with yourself, be in love with each other, be in love with life.

The meaning of love is not only for the romantic. The meaning of love is powerful and when experienced love has no limits. We can literally love everyone that we meet. Love has no boundaries. When we are in love's presence we have no fear. When we embrace love without limitations, prejudice, and judgment it has the powerful to change us and everyone in the universe. At the same time, when we are in love's embrace we don't have to feel lonely because love eliminates the sense of loneliness and separation. I can be in love as well I can love from wherever I am. We love from the grace of the spirit not from our desires to love.

We are prevented from loving others when our judgments of another person overshadow our minds. Judgments can lead to anger, resentment, hatred, and frustration for us and for others. Take for example, someone from a different background than yourself, are you capable of love for this person. The answer is yes. What prevents us from experiencing love for others is our prejudging. What makes you judge that person? It is probably a lack of unconditional love. Our conditioned thoughts and behaviors about other people get in our way of experiencing the kind of love that Paul talks about in Corinthians.

Love has many qualities. First, love is **unconditional**. When we love completely we place no limitations or conditions of our love. We set the other person free by allowing that person to simply be who they are. Our love is not dependent on someone else's behavior but it sees past the faults of others. Second, love is ***complete acceptance*** of another. To allow people to be exactly who they are is the best part of love; to have no limitations or expectations, just a true genuine, I love you. How amazing when we accept each other as we are, with our seemingly flaws and all. Third, love is ***selfless***. True love asks nothing in return. When our parents raise us to become the wonderful people that we are, they don't say at the end, you owe me my child. Parents usually have a complete and total selfless love for their children. Parents love for the sake of loving. When we love our lovers we love for the sake of being in love and we expect nothing in return.

To harness the power of love and increase it in your life, talk only about love, imagine only love, embrace only love, see only love, become only love. Never underestimate the power of love. The power of love has no bounds and we can change the world with the power of love. When we show only love and not be reminded of what we don't love we can easily change the world around us. My life was completely transformed when I began to love those around me with a love that is unselfish and unconditional.

To know the full meaning of life is to know love; the greatest force on earth. We came here not to find ourselves but to love each other and love life. The reason that we have a hard time loving each other is because of conditioning. Our basic nature is love. We have more love that we can ever know. Start living your life today by first finding your way home; that is, your way back to love. There is a place that cannot be explained and that place is love. Speak only love, feel only love, share only love, think only about love, make love your purpose in life. When you talk only about love you are creating the greatest vibration in the universe. Love is all that is permanent in this life and it is the one power that we can harness to change our life. A genuine, heartfelt, and warm type of love is literally life supporting. When we love from our true essence of divinity the world becomes transformed. We have the power to change our lives and those around us by being in love with life.

Apply the Key of Love

1) Practice only love in all that you do. Practice love in all of your thoughts and actions.

2) Find the best in others, try not to change people but love them as they are.

3) Make love a priority by talking only about what you love and don't talk about the things that you don't love.

4) Fall in love with life and stay there; it's the greatest place in the universe.

Conclusion

The potential for joy in this time space reality is beyond anything anyone has ever seen –Abraham Hicks

You have within you the most amazing power to transform your life. This power is available to each of us and is available at any time that we choose to summons it into action. We have to know that we can tap into and harness this power at any time and for any purpose. The purpose of our lives is pure joy and pure love. Your life will begin to change in that moment when you realize just how powerful you are. You can have all your wishes fulfilled the moment that you believe that you can have it. You are meant to be happy and to live an amazing life. You are meant to have all the things that you desire. What you want, wants you. What you think about, you attract. Believe in the power of your mind to change your life. Set aside once and for all the thoughts that you are hopeless over the circumstances of your life. You are more powerful than you can imagine. You can begin, starting today, live the life of your dreams.

Within this book are the keys to unlocking your potential to an amazing life. Each key provides practical solutions that will inspire, encourage, and motivate you to a profound change in your life.

When you change the way that you see things, the things you see will change.

The first key, the **key of awareness** inspires us to become aware of who we really are, where we are in our current awareness as a person, and what we have been conditioned by those around us to believe about ourselves. Awareness is the first step or action we must make in order to make significant changes in our life. There first need to be the awareness that you need or want to change. When I find myself in a place where it has become hard or difficult for me to achieve a goal, I simply put my intention out to the universe about what it is I hope to achieve. Awareness sets things in motion. It allows us to take the necessary steps as well as it allows the universal forces of the law of attraction to manifest our dreams and unlock the key to our highest potentials.

The second key, the **key of belief** is our attitude that we have about ourselves. Your belief can be one of limitations or it can hold the key to amazing potential in your life. You see our thoughts are things and what we believe to be true will in fact be so. In order to change your life and unlock your potential you must change what you deeply believe about yourself. What you believe about yourself to be true will indeed be true for you. What are some of the deep abiding truths that you hold about yourself? Are they truths to prosper you or are they truths that are destroying your life.

The third key, the **key of attention**; remember that what we place our attention on grows. Where attention goes, the life grows; thus it becomes so important where we put our mental focus. If I am thinking about positive things in my life, then my life will be positive. If I am thinking about negative things in my life, then my life will be negative. Thoughts are everything and where you place your attention is what will be manifested in your life. You are what your deep driving desire is; therefore, as you think so shall you be.

The fourth key, the **key of transformation** is where all possibilities can take place. When you become aware of who you are and you know who you are you magically begin to transform your life into all possibilities. You have the power to transform your life into anything that you can imagine is possible. Your personal transformation is your opportunity for unlocking your highest potential.

The fifth key, the **key of awakening** is where you find your purpose. You have a real purpose in life; you have come here with some special gift to give to the world. When you awake to this purpose you will begin to see that everything that you do is for your higher good. You finally realize that everything that you ever needed or wanted in your life is available to you at any moment. The awaken soul sees all, hears all, and knows all. The awaken soul does only what is good for their life.

The sixth key, the **key of gratitude** is when you are in a place of gratefulness, appreciation, and thankfulness for all that show up in your life. Gratitude is when what you say is in alignment with what you do and how you treat those around you.

The seventh key, the **key of love,** is the place at which you start to live your amazing life. Love is the strongest force in the universe. It is the cause of all that is good in your life. When you come from a place of love in all that you say and do your life becomes an unlimited source and you live your true divinity.

The Seven Keys to Unlocking Your potential are key principles; when applied can lead you to a process of reflection, enlightenment, and thanksgiving that will help you to transform your life. If you can place these practices deep into your sub consciousness you will begin to see and witness miracles in your life. The key to achieving greatness is within your reach. If you can understand why you are here and what you showed up to do, you will be able to understand and achieve anything you want. Love is the highest force in the universe. Begin to experience it today and to spread it to all those that you come into contact with.

Made in the USA
Middletown, DE
09 February 2015